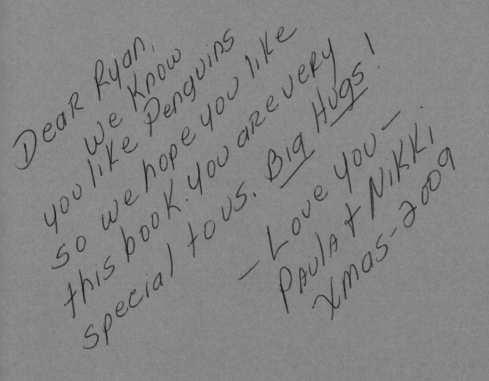

Dear Ryan,
we know
you like Penguins
so we hope you like
this book. You are very
special to us. Big Hugs!
— Love you—
Paula + Nikki
Xmas-2009

PENGUIN LIFE

SURVIVING WITH STYLE
IN THE SOUTH ATLANTIC

**ANDY ROUSE
& TRACEY RICH**

**BARNES
& NOBLE**

NEW YORK

ISBN-13: 978-1-4351-0409-9
ISBN-10: 1-4351-0409-9

Printed and bound in Singapore

10 9 8 7 6 5 4 3 2 1

CONTENTS

INTRODUCTION

Flightless, and frequenting some of the most inhospitable regions on Earth, penguins are undoubtedly the most recognizable and enigmatic characters of the frozen south. There are some 17 different species of this remarkable bird – those featured here lead fascinating lives in and around the coasts and rocks of sub-Antarctica and its peninsula. They are the Kings, Gentoos, Rockhoppers, Chinstraps and Adélies, who dive, surf, fight, play, breed, feed, swap partners and rock climb their way through life.

Penguins have adopted some of the coldest and most inaccessible niches of the Antarctic Peninsula and the sub-Antarctic Islands that surround the frozen mainland. From the coasts of South America to those of New Zealand and even South Africa, penguins have found homes where few of us have the opportunity to visit. Only really able to follow them on land, we get an unbalanced view of the penguin – one which is of a cumbersome and somewhat daft creature collecting stones to make nests and standing in all weathers balancing eggs on their feet. However, what we often don't see is the grace and speed with which they swim and fish, the dedication they have to their chicks, the miraculous feats of agility they perform getting to and from the sea and the harsh environments and hazards they have to outwit in their daily lives.

Penguin Life is an extraordinary insight into the lesser-known areas of penguins' lives. Witnessed by living alongside them in their world, the images presented in this book are first-hand glimpses into the comings and goings of penguins as they go about their daily routines of courtship, bringing up chicks and growing up in the frozen seas of the sub-Antarctic.

The culmination of many years spent sitting with our penguin friends, watching, waiting and laughing at them, the images clearly show the trials of life these creatures encounter in the most southerly reaches of the globe. Photographing penguins is an incredibly rewarding experience – they are the epitome of good looks in their distinctive black 'tail coats' and 'white shirt fronts', as polar explorer Apsley Cherry-Garrard, a member of Scott's ill-fated polar expedition of 1910–12, described them in his 1922 account of the voyage, *The Worst Journey in the World*. Our visits to Antarctica have been considerably more enjoyable than his, and were made all the better by the spectacular sights we managed to photograph there, which we now share with you.

Their distinctive flashes of colour make penguins immediately identifiable, as do their peculiar habits and astonishing ability for doing the unthinkable, such as climbing sheer rock faces and finding their way back to their single chick amongst 500,000 other penguins. Each and every one of them has a personality as distinct as our own, even if they do all look the same to untrained eyes. Spend long enough in their company, however, and you can soon see who fancies whom, who are the shy and retiring types and who are the more raucous, and who simply can't keep their adolescent offspring on the straight and narrow.

Our experiences of penguins have left a lasting impression on us. For despite the fact that their lives are undeniably tough – living in the frozen seas of Antarctica with everything from the cold, exposure, whales, sealions, pollution, human disturbance, climate change and even other birds trying to destroy them – penguins know how to have fun and do not fail to bring a smile to your face with their eccentric antics and clown-like behaviour.

We hope that through our pictures we can bring some of that fun and amusement to you too, and you might just find that there is far more to penguins than you ever imagined.

Andy Rouse & Tracey Rich

PENGUINLIFE

In the southern-most oceans of the world, penguins live out their orderly and regimented lives on the rugged coastlines of tiny islands and the outermost reaches of the great frozen continent that is Antarctica. From cheeky rock climbers to aloof royalty, the lives of these black-and-white wonders are far from monochrome. Come and discover the secret lives of penguins ...

◄ A PORTUGESE DISCOVERY

One of the most unusual penguin species in the sub-Antarctic Islands is the Magellanic. The name refers to the Portuguese explorer, Ferdinand Magellan who, in 1519, was the first person to attempt the circumnavigation of the globe. Sadly, he did not make it and the dreadful conditions he and his sailors endured meant that another attempt did not occur until Sir Francis Drake's expedition in 1577. Many geographical features retain the name Magellan in the south Americas, in particular the Magellan Straits, which pass between mainland South America and Tierra del Fuego.

THE DISTINCTIVE ADELIE ▷

The Adélie penguin is unmistakable, with its distinctive white eye rings and flattened shape to the head. Adélie penguins also gain their name from another pioneering navigator, this time Frenchman Dumont d'Urville, who named them after his wife.

◀ CRESTED ROCKHOPPERS

Rockhopper penguins cannot claim such illustrious forbears to their name as Adélies – it derives simply from one of their most outstanding traits. Rockhoppers are familiar to many as they are often found in zoological collections. They are a member of the 'crested' penguins, i.e. those with strange golden hairstyles, which also include the oddly-named Macaroni and the Royal penguin.

AN ADELIE PENGUIN COMES ASHORE ▶

Incidentally, the famous British polar explorer Sir Ernest Shackleton also named one of his daughters Adélie.

013

SLEEPING KING PENGUIN ▶
When chance allows, penguins sleep just like any other bird, by placing their head under their wing. Penguins will only sleep when they are in a group so that there is always someone keeping an eye out in case of trouble.

◀ A KING PENGUIN SHOWS OFF HIS MAJESTY

Despite their size, on average around 95cm (37in) tall, and the fact that they form large breeding colonies of hundreds of thousands of individuals, King penguins are very sensitive to disturbance and must be approached with caution. Kings move in a typically regal way with an elegant, unhurried walk while observing their surroundings with a sideways glance, always ensuring that their beaks are held high.

▲ WATERPROOFING FOR WARMTH

Preening is an important part of penguin life, as it is for any other sea-going animal or bird. Salty water is not good for the maintenance of feathers, so water- and weather-proofing them is essential in such a cold and harsh climate to ensure that the feathers are kept in tiptop condition to keep the birds warm and dry.

ROCKHOPPER PENGUINS TAKING A SHOWER

These penguins are taking it in turns to shower under the freshwater waterfalls on their return to land from fishing out at sea. Not only does the fresh water help to rid their feathers of salt deposits but it is likely that, in comparison to the freezing sea, the freshwater from the land is like stepping into a hot bath before going to bed. Watching carefully, the penguins certainly seemed to enjoy themselves in the shower and there were plenty of arguments between them when individuals had spent too long in a favourite spot.

◄◄ GENTOO PENGUINS ON A FLOATING BERG
We normally think of penguins living on the ice but as this book shows, the vast majority of penguins live on the peripheries of mainland Antarctica, which can be free of snow and ice for much of the year. Gentoo penguins seldom venture further than 65-degrees south. The only places they are likely to encounter ice are the erratic floating bergs of the Antarctic Peninsula or in the waters in which they feed.

◄ A FINE BLACK LINE
Chinstrap penguins are more at home around icebound areas, but they can equally be found on ice-free sub-Antarctic islands, and also on the frozen continent itself. Their name is derived simply from the fine black line that passes under their chin which is reminiscent of a chinstrap holding on a helmet or ceremonial hat.

WHAT'S IN A NAME? ►
The name Gentoo has far more ambiguous origins. The word 'gentoo' does have precedence in the Hindustani word for 'pagan', which may have come from early settlers and explorers in the Antarctic and sub-Antarctic areas. Part of the Gentoo's scientific name (*Pygoscelis papua*) 'papua' comes from the mistaken belief that the penguins originally came from Papua New Guinea.

DOZING CHINSTRAP ▶

Penguins have some of the most attractive personalities of any birds, probably as they often remind us of ourselves. This sleepy Chinstrap is no exception. By nature, penguins have little fear of mammals on land, except on the beach – their main predators are at sea or are other birds. Consequently, penguins have inquisitive natures and have no direct fear of humans, which allows us to get a rare and privileged insight into their world at close quarters, on land at least.

INSIDE A WAVE ▶▶

This Gentoo penguin is actually peering at you from inside a wave! Penguins find human visitors endlessly fascinating and their curiosity makes them very endearing. The distinctive markings on the face and body of penguins make them relatively easy to identify, presumably to other penguin species as well as to ourselves.

▲▶ LEAPING CHINSTRAPS

Emerging from frozen waters can be difficult when you have short legs and flippers. Unless there is a shallow incline out of the water, penguins will often jump directly onto rocks as these Chinstrap penguins are doing. Presumably the layer of insulating blubber that all penguins have also helps them to bounce when they occasionally misjudge their landing.

◀ BALANCING ACT

Being flightless is no hindrance to penguins, who have evolved a form of underwater flight. They are somewhat cumbersome on land however, as their short and stumpy legs have evolved for steering like rudders, rather than for hill-walking. This doesn't stop most penguins though, who do walk considerable distances with vast amounts of effort. Their wings, or rather flippers, are used for balance, giving them their characteristic waddle when walking on land.

◀ MAJESTIC KINGS

King penguins are the sleek and streamlined executive penguin model, both in water and on land. They have long flippers and an upright stance, and look a bit like they are wearing an over-long coat when they walk. They use their long and slender bills to great effect, both as a fine preening tool and occasionally as a weapon against rivals.

A GENTOO PENGUIN AT SUNSET ▶

Gentoo penguins belong to a group called the brush tails, for obvious reasons. The brush tails also include the Adélie and Chinstrap penguins. They all prefer breeding sites that are on exposed island slopes and make their nests out of stones, twigs and shale.

◄◄ A CHINSTRAP SOAKS UP THE SUN

Penguins like nothing more than sunbathing when they have just emerged from the icy depths of the sea and you'll often see them standing facing the sun with their flippers outstretched. If you watch closely you can see the colour gradually return to their feet (if they are pale like this Chinstrap penguin). In a similar manner to a dog, they will shake the water free from their bodies as soon as they are out of the water, thus re-establishing the insulating properties of their feathers.

◄ MAGELLANIC BURROWERS

In the cold and windswept sub-Antarctic islands, such as the Falkland Islands, Magellanic penguins have the added benefit of living inside a burrow. Much like a rabbit warren, areas where there are many penguins can quickly become like a golf course – albeit one with an awful lot of bunkers.

GOLDEN GLOW ▶

The Rockhopper penguin also enjoys the sun, particularly at the end the day when the light is beautiful and shows up its stunning blood-red eye and sharp stubby beak, which is a powerful weapon. Despite being small (2.5–3.5kg/5½–7¾lbs and only a maximum of 58cm/23in tall), the Rockhopper is generally quite an aggressive character, lacking fear of other penguins and being nonplussed by humans too.

HOMELIFE

Despite our preconceptions, the vast majority of the 17 penguin species do not live or breed on ice. They frequent some of the most inhospitable and remote areas of the Southern Hemisphere but can be found on sand, rocks, grass, shale, terminal moraine, in freshwater, on cliffs, among industrial debris and on mountainsides. Wherever you find a penguin, you will see a species that has adapted its lifestyle to cope with its chosen home environment.

◀ FALKLAND COLONIES

Penguins can have a significant impact on their local environment, especially during the breeding season when they gather in large colonies. The colonies shown in this image, taken in the Falkland Islands, are unusual in that they are mixed species of Rockhoppers and King Cormorants. These species are often found nesting alongside each other, and while there is little explanation as to why, it must be for some mutual benefit – perhaps safety in numbers or purely due to limited suitable nesting sites.

▲ GENTOO BREEDING SITES

Each penguin species tends to prefer a slightly different habitat in which to breed. Gentoos are most frequently found on smooth rocks, pebbles and shale. They are also attracted to areas of short tussac grass, the remnants of which can often be seen trampled and filthy with muck in and around the breeding colony.

◀ ON THE ROCKS WITH ROCKHOPPERS

Rockhoppers, as their name suggests, prefer a more rugged habitat, often nesting on steep and sheer cliffs. It is remarkable that they lay and incubate their eggs, and raise their young in such a precarious location.

◀ UPWIND APPROACH

Gentoo penguins form large colonies and you can often smell them long before you see them. The stench has an unbelievable power of pervasion – despite washing the smell lingers in your hair and clothes for days afterwards.
The trick to this is to approach the colony from upwind.

A BREEDING PAIR OF MAGELLANICS ▶

Magellanic penguins are always found in places where there is soft sand or peaty soil in which to excavate their burrows. These areas are often located further inland than other penguin colonies, meaning that the Magellanic has to run the gauntlet of angry parents in other colonies on their way to and from their home.

◀◀ ENVIRONMENTAL IMPACT

With concentrations of many hundreds of birds in one place, inevitably there are vast quantities of guano (penguin droppings) deposited in the local environment. Here, at a remote colony on the Aitcho Islands (part of the South Shetlands group), you can clearly see the patches of white penguin droppings painting the landscape in a dramatic fashion.

◀ TAKING SHELTER IN A FORMER WHALING SITE

Many sub-Antarctic islands were formerly used in the whaling industry, and the infrastructure of rusting machinery and buildings has been left behind, long after the industry has died. Penguins have re-colonized these areas, utilizing decaying buildings as shelter, like these King penguins on South Georgia.

◀ GENTOO PENGUINS FISHING

Gentoo penguins are one of the most widespread of penguin species and, when they are not breeding, spend most of their time around the winter pack ice and close to their colony. Gentoos prefer to make their colonies near the shoreline. Here, we can see Gentoos behaving like domesticated ducks. They spend much time dabbling in shallow waters for food during the breeding season but also use these waters for bathing too. The alternative name for the Gentoo, Johnny penguin, clearly illustrates that early settlers saw Gentoos as familiar and commonplace.

WEIGHING IN ▶

You will never see a thin penguin. The reason for this is that all penguins, like the mammals that share their Antarctic habitats, are covered with a liberal layer of blubber. As penguins have evolved so that they do not fly, they are freed from the constraints of weight and so can afford to be a little fatter. The blubber in itself is a buoyancy aid in the water as well as providing the birds with insulation.

MUCK AND MAGIC ▶

With large numbers of birds within the colony, they are mucky places to be and it is essential for the birds to clean themselves off before embarking on a fishing expedition. Dirty plumage means poor insulation and waterproofing, which is to be avoided when you are about to spend time in one of the coldest marine environments in the world.

▼ SHY BUT NOT SO RETIRING

Magellanic penguins are a constant source of amusement. Despite their shy personalities when humans are around, they are in fact insatiably curious and it doesn't take long for them to re-emerge from their burrows to take another look.

VULNERABLE ROCKHOPPERS ▶

Rockhoppers are tough little penguins, but they are in decline and are classified as 'vulnerable' under the International Union for the Conservation of Nature and Natural Resources (IUCN) listings. Very few actually breed in the Southern Ocean and their distribution remains predominantly north of the polar front. Rockhoppers, as their name suggests, are found on the edges of islands, clinging onto the rough and exposed cliff ledges often alongside albatrosses and cormorants, which are characteristic of more northerly areas of the Antarctic region.

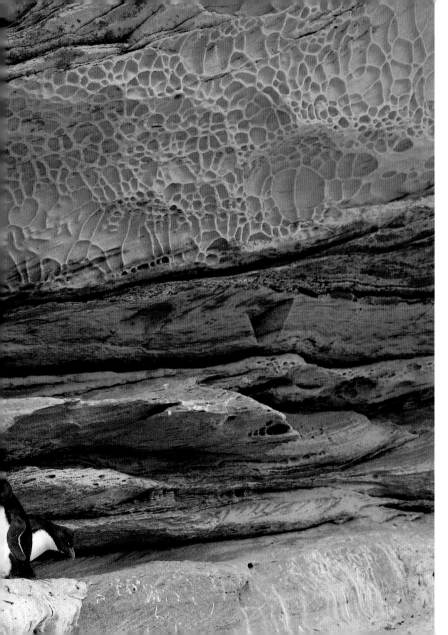

▼ A FEARLESS BUNCH

Even high-up on the tops of cliffs you will find a group of Rockhoppers trotting by. Their fearless nature means that if you sit quietly and patiently they will often come to you, even pecking your boots if you sit still enough.

NATURAL SCULPTURE

This image illustrates the real meaning of the name Rockhopper. Even in areas where humans can't climb, Rockhopper penguins are able to scale the heights using their finely clawed feet. Here you can see the scrapes and scratches that thousands of sharp claws have made on the rock face over many generations.

ROCKHOPPER ROOKERY ▷

A Rockhopper colony on the Falkland Islands. They are busy places but not quite as dirty or smelly as many other penguin colonies. Despite their small size, Rockhoppers walk and climb many hundreds of metres up and down the cliffs, and to and from the shore.

◀ WHICH WAY IS HOME?
This King penguin looks a little lost and occasionally when returning to the breeding colony individuals do go astray. Prevailing weather conditions can affect the birds' navigational abilities and this may be of considerable concern in the future with the likely effects of global climate change.

◀ NIGHTLY ROUTINE
Penguins remain on land at night, sleeping periodically while standing or lying down on their bellies. With a lack of land predators, except on the beaches, adult penguins are reasonably safe at night – their greatest threat comes from the cold and exposure

PENGUIN NICHES ▶

Penguins inhabit similar environments but different ecological niches. With little competition from other bird species, penguins are able to flourish whether on ice or on sandy beaches.

◀ ADELIES FROM THE AIR

Adélies prefer to be further south than many other penguin species and often breed on the mainland, exposing them to a cooler climate and therefore slightly different diets. Penguins are known to modify their diets according to local variations.

◀ A BLANKET EFFECT
Penguins are gregarious birds and when in their breeding colonies during the austral (Southern Hemisphere) summer, their numbers can be considerable, covering the landscape in a blanket of black and white. Gentoo penguins prefer a slightly sloping aspect that catches the morning light.

SEAS OF KINGS ON SOUTH GEORGIA ▶
South Georgia boasts two or three locations that attract huge numbers of King penguins. The reason for this is possibly the lack of suitable sites – much of the island is surrounded by high, vertical cliffs and mountain slopes that are too steep even for Rockhoppers to climb. They remain the reserves of seabirds such as albatrosses that have not lost the ability to fly, while the penguins stay closer to the shore.

◀ HALF A MILLION KING PENGUINS

Evocatively named Salisbury Plain and St Andrew's Bay by pioneering British explorers, the main locations for the biggest breeding colonies of King penguins are quite unlike anything else in the world. With upwards of 500,000 individuals, it is impossible to see the ground at all and even the glacial river is lined with penguins – some even have to stand in the water as there is no room left on dry land.

A ROYAL PAIR ▶

The breeding colonies of penguins on South Georgia are so vast that they even start to creep up the mountainsides that surround the bay. This pair has chosen an elevated spot above the hustle and bustle of the main colony.

FAMILY LIFE

The drive to reproduce is as strong in penguins as it is in any other creature. The short summer in the far south means that they must come together and get down to business as quickly as possible in order to raise their young to a stage where they can survive a frozen winter. For penguins the race is on, leading to a frenetic period in their lives

◀ TWO-DAY OLD GENTOO CHICKS

The rate at which penguin chicks grow is almost solely dependent on their parents' ability to fish. These chicks were only a couple of days old when they were photographed, but they reached the size of the chick shown opposite just over a week or so later.

A GENTOO CHICK GETS A MEAL ▷

Gentoo penguins lay two eggs and normally raise two chicks, especially on the Peninsula. Gentoos feed in shallow areas close to the colony and it is probable that this is one of the reasons why they are so successful and less likely to abandon their eggs or chicks.

YOUNG KING PENGUIN AND PARENT ▶▶▶

In complete contrast to the stunning elegance of the adult King penguin, the young are real ugly ducklings. In fact when explorers first visited the islands surrounding Antarctica, they were convinced that they were a separate species altogether. Old reports state that there was a brown species of penguin called the Woolly penguin.

AN ENORMOUS EFFORT ▶▶

Woolly penguins are actually the King penguins' year-old chicks from the previous breeding season. The penguins are restricted in the number of offspring they can raise because of their size and ability to feed such ravenous youngsters. Due to the immense effort that goes into rearing their young, the King penguin breeds on a three-year cycle, as it often takes two breeding seasons to successfully raise one chick.

AN EGG ON ITS FEET ▶

Like its cousin, the Emperor penguin, (which breeds in colonies on the edges of the mainland of the southern continent) the King penguin lays one large egg which is immediately manoeuvred onto the feet, away from the freezing ground and protected by the overhanging brood patch. This is a fold of skin with well developed blood supply. It effectively works as an electric blanket to keep the egg warm. They do not build nests in these harsh environments – with the ever-present howling gales they would simply blow away.

◀ LEARNING BY IMITATION
Magellanic penguins are raised in the comparative luxury of a nice, warm burrow. Attended by both parents they quickly become confident and try to imitate their parents at the burrow's entrance.

▲ FEEDING TIME
Feeding youngsters is a never-ending battle for penguin parents. They never seem to deliver food in sufficient quantities or frequently enough for their growing offspring. There is always a sense of urgency about feeding time, because there is only a small window of opportunity before youngsters have to be strong enough to cope with the harsh realities of winter in the sub-Antarctic.

▲ PARENT-CHICK RECOGNITION
Chicks of all species are programmed to beg for food from any adult penguin that comes near. It is astonishing how the chicks are able to recognize their own parents amongst the chaotic mass of birds that are to-ing and fro-ing in the colony. The act is believed to be assisted by voice recognition, which in reality is a combination of squeaks, whistles and wheezes.

A YOUNG KING PENGUIN DURING MOULTING ▷

After regaining the weight they lost during the winter period, young King penguins moult out into their juvenile plumage, which is simply a paler version of the adult's. It must be a very itchy time of year and when part way through the process the birds can look completely ridiculous.

▲ **SHARED PARENTAL RESPONSIBILITY**
Both parents take turns in incubating the egg, feeding the young
and undertaking guard duty. The chick will encourage the
parent to regurgitate its food by pecking at the lower mandible
– presumably the colourful bill helps them to hit the target.

As part of their development, the young will mimic the actions and behaviours of the adults including trying to call, as this Gentoo chick is attempting.

▲ GENTOO CHICKS STICK TOGETHER
Staying together ensures that the young are more protected and they can also keep warm by huddling in close. Chicks can also be observed playing together, running around and flexing their flippers in a strange game of kiss-chase.

◀ KING PENGUIN CHICKS IN A CRECHE
Crèches are formed by most species of penguin. Why a crèche is formed is a matter of some debate. It may be a result of the adult penguins' aggression towards their adolescent offspring, or simply a safe place to leave them when out fishing.

◄ MAGELLANIC CHICK AND ADULT
Magellanic penguin chicks are less gregarious than most and stick tightly to their parents' side, quickly growing to become as big as the adults.

◄ AN ATTENTIVE PARENT
Some species of chicks quickly begin to look like their parents while others, like this Rockhopper, have a long way to go. They are vigorously protected by their parents because at this stage they are at their most vulnerable to predators such as the Skua and Striated Caracara, as well as exposure to the elements.

YOUNG GENTOOS GAINING INDEPENDENCE ►
After the crèche stage and once they are large enough, most young penguins move further and further away from the colony and their parents. They usually venture towards the sea, tentatively dabbling in the water as they learn to swim.

A KING PENGUIN MID-MOULT

Every year King penguins need to renew their feathers to ensure that they are fully waterproofed and insulated for the winter weather ahead. After breeding they begin to moult – the ground becomes covered in feathers and resembles the aftermath of an enormous pillow fight.

AS FAR AS THE EYE CAN SEE ▶

With so many penguins in one place, you can imagine the volume of muck and feathers that they leave behind. Note the distinct brown patches in the sea of King penguins – these are the crèches of youngsters.

◄ DUSK CHORUS
As dusk falls there is a brief period of calling and frantic activity in the colony. Youngsters will try to call like their parents but have yet to master the tuneful trumpeting of the adults ... and then the colony falls silent.

PARENTAL GUIDANCE ▷
The parent of this young Gentoo chick stands guard over it as it flexes its flippers, gradually building up the muscle strength it needs to become a strong swimmer.

067

◀ **JUVENILE GENTOOS NEARING ADULTHOOD**
As Gentoo chicks mature, it rapidly becomes difficult to tell the difference between the chicks and their parents.

▼ **WINDOW OF OPPORTUNITY**
Gentoo chicks join the crèche at around a month old and are ready to go to sea at about three-and-a-half months old. The short austral summer means that penguins must develop quickly in order to be strong enough for the winter.

◀ YOUNG GENTOOS PRACTISE SURFING
Their first experience of the sea tends to be in gangs of juveniles, who bravely enter the water and inelegantly body surf back onto the beach.

ADELIE CHICKS DISCOVER SNOW ▶
Despite the Adélie's liking for ice they cannot lay their eggs until their chosen nesting area is free of snow. Once old enough however, youngsters are guided by adults onto the snow for the first time.

SUCCESS AT THE CENTRE ▶
It is often true that the most successful penguin parents take up the central positions within the colony and will return there year after year – presumably this is because it affords greater protection not only from predators but also from extremes in temperature.

◀ MAGELLANIC CHICKS PREPARE FOR THEIR FIRST DIP
Being brought up in the safety of a burrow makes Magellanic youngsters particularly nervous when in wide open spaces on the beach. This crèche of juveniles huddle together tightly as they venture tentatively into the surf for the first time.

COMMUTERLIFE

The daily grind of going to work in the morning and returning after a hard day is not confined to our own urban way of life. Many penguin species also undertake a daily trudge to 'work' and home again before dusk. A matter of survival in the Sub-Antarctic, these daily migrations are carefully choreographed and coordinated to ensure the best

SAFETY IN NUMBERS

One of the most difficult parts of a penguin's daily routine is the transition in and out of the sea. It is here where they are most at risk from predators and so their arrival and departure is highly synchronized.

ROCKHOPPER DEXTERITY

If you do not believe that penguins can rock climb, here is evidence to prove it. With sharp claws and an incredibly strong little body, the Rockhopper has made this a speciality, climbing up rocks that even humans might find difficult using both our hands and feet. Getting down is somewhat easier, though.

▼ ROCKHOPPERS CLIMB UP TO THEIR NEST SITE

Rockhoppers may climb great distances to their nesting sites up steep cliffs rising directly from the sea. They are site faithful, meaning that they return to the same nesting site time and time again. Presumably, the scarcity of suitable sites means that this is a more important resource than who their mate is, therefore Rockhoppers do not necessarily mate with the same individual every year.

▲ GENTOOS TAKING A BEACH BREAK
Penguins gather closely on the beach as they return from a fishing expedition before making their way inland. They will often pause for a rest, if safe to do so, prior to gathering in sufficient numbers to wind their way back to the colony.

◀ ROCKHOPPERS ON THE MARCH
The further inland the penguins get the more likely they are to spread out, and long lines of marching penguins can be seen strewn across the beach, hillside or rock face.

MAKING A DASH FOR IT ▶
Rockhoppers favour highly difficult landing sites, which often means an undignified arrival on the rocks. To prevent being swept back to sea by the next wave, they often have to make a quick dash up the rocks and out of harm's way.

CHILLING OUT

Specialists in feeding on crustaceans and especially krill, Chinstrap penguins concentrate their feeding efforts just below the surface of the sea where it is warmest and most productive. When they need a rest during the day they will hop up onto nearby icebergs as they are agile climbers.

ASSERTIVE ACTION

Despite their diminutive size – the third smallest penguin in the world – the Rockhopper is an assertive character and will ensure that it assumes right of way when moving to and from its colony site. By forming small 'gangs' Rockhoppers will actively dispute a right of way with any other species found blocking their path, even humans.

QUICK MARCH

Once underway, Rockhoppers are unlikely to stop on their procession back to the colony, undertaking a swift march like tiny soldiers.

ROCKHOPPERS EMERGE FROM THE SEA▼

Probably the most robust of all the penguins, these tiny
Rockhoppers show just how tough they are by emerging
onto the rocks amidst the crashing waves.

THE CHINSTRAP HIGHWAY ▶

Climbing up steep slopes of ice is not easy even when you
are a Chinstrap penguin; who are specialists in this area.
Over the course of the breeding season the snow and ice is
so well trodden by commuting penguins that deep runways
are formed. Over time these become stained with dirt,
guano and tinted pink with regurgitated krill.

◀◀ ▲▲ **ROCKHOPPERS MAKING AN UNUSUAL RETURN**
Rockhoppers clambering through seaweed fronds on the rocky
shores ... and unusually arriving on a sandy beach, only to make
their way directly towards the steepest cliffs nearby where their
colony is located alongside the albatrosses.

▲ DAWN PATROL
Just after dawn, penguins are in a hurry to get out into the sea to fish. With only a limited amount of daylight as they are seen here, the pressure is on to eat as much as possible before returning at dusk.

◀ RUSH HOUR – ANTARCTIC STYLE
The arrival of penguins ashore at the end of the day is an important time. With hungry chicks to feed in the colony there is a sense of urgency to get home.

◀ A PENGUIN'S DIET
Penguins tend to specialize in particular types of prey, from crustaceans and and squid to fish and plankton. All penguins are carnivores. On returning from a successful day's fishing, their bellies are noticeably more round than when they left the colony earlier in the morning.

NAVIGATION TECHNIQUES ▶
It is thought that penguins navigate principally by using the sun, their path home being more direct when it is not cloudy.

▲ GOING SOLO
During the breeding season in the austral spring and summer, penguins will often take it in turns to fish and undertake nesting duties. Parents may swap roles several times a day and there will often be a constant stream of birds arriving or leaving the colony and making their way to the sea.

◀ RITUAL MIGRATION

The migration to and from colonies, or 'rookeries' as they are known, has been engrained in penguins for hundreds, if not thousands of years. Sites are seldom abandoned; those that have been deserted are most likely to have been subject to changes in climate, and therefore abundance of food, or have been disturbed by human encroachment – the two main factors that threaten penguin survival.

▼ THE FIRST ONE

There always has to be the first penguin to enter the sea every morning. At sunrise the urge to go and fish is strong and eventually this instinct outweighs the potential hazards such as sealions waiting in the surf.

SOCIALLIFE

Penguins are experts at communal living – they have to be, as living in such hostile environments they rely on each other to survive. However, that doesn't mean to say that they always get on with their neighbours and when it comes to finding a mate and raising offspring, squabbles between individuals and families are frequent.

KING PENGUINS IN CONFERENCE ▷
Colony life means that penguins spend considerable
amounts of time together, roughing it out in the difficult
weather conditions experienced in the southern seas.
Whether huddling together for warmth or simply hanging
out with friends, penguins are always in the company
of others – it does make you wonder exactly what it is
that they find to talk about.

Sitting among the Gentoo penguin colonies on the Falkland Islands is one of the greatest privileges we have had. Towards dusk they will instantaneously begin a raucous round of calling, by throwing their heads back in the air as if star-gazing, while letting out an ear-piercing yet tuneful note or two. Youngsters also copy their parents – often not quite so in tune but they do give it all that they've got.

◀ AN ADULT GENTOO PENGUIN CALLING
Here is an adult Gentoo penguin calling during the day.
Whether or not this is a territorial or a bonding activity within
the colony we do not know, but the activity is performed
sporadically throughout the day by parents and their young,
culminating in a whole colony performance towards dusk.

GENTOO PENGUINS ON THE ROCKS ▶
Preferring ice-free areas of the sub-Antarctic to breed,
Gentoos can be found in a number of different habitats
but often on rocks. These rocks are stained with many years
of guano build-up. Note the Chinstrap penguins who have
joined in with this group.

▶ ROCKHOPPER DISPUTE

With hairstyles resembling punk rockers, Rockhoppers are known to be highly aggressive towards each other and other species sharing their area. Squabbles between Rockhoppers are frequent and, armed with strong, sharp beaks they look as though they could give a nasty nip if provoked. Here, two are arguing about who should go first in the shower.

▼ PERSONAL SPACE

Just like humans, penguins have friends and foes too. Loud squawking and the occasional jab from a very sharp beak is usually enough to reinforce the point if someone gets too close for comfort.

◀ LOCATION, LOCATION, LOCATION

The locations of colonies may not be determined directly by the precise surroundings on land but by the surrounding underwater geography. Proximity to shallow and thus warmer and more productive waters in which to feed, are believed to be important factors for where penguins choose to place their colonies.

◄ THREE'S A CROWD

Underlying this serene scene of three King penguins walking on a pristine beach at sunrise, is a more significant behaviour – that of courtship. It is the breeding season for King penguins during the austral spring and summer.

KING PENGUIN RIVALRY ▶

Although it is difficult to tell males from females among most penguin species, their behaviour during the breeding season will often give their sex away. This image shows a male King penguin fending off another rival with his flipper. The female lurking close behind him is surely encouraging him.

◀ **TAKING A BREAK**
Even in the coldest reaches of the sub-Antarctic Islands and the Peninsula, penguins are never found on their own unless they are in trouble. Small groups are often found resting and warming up on icebergs during fishing trips.

THREE GENTOOS REST ON AN ICEBERG ▶
Sitting high-up on this beautiful blue iceberg, three Gentoo penguins rest and warm themselves in the weak Antarctic haze, which passes for sunshine during the austral summer. They do not find it easy walking on ice and will sometimes resort to sliding on their bellies over longer distances. They jump feet first from the edge of the iceberg when returning to the sea.

◄ MUTUAL SUPPORT

Rockhoppers have one of the most precarious challenges getting to and from their colonies, and they appear to gather together for support and encouragement before leaping into the unknown when going out to sea.

KING PENGUINS COURTING ▶

The mating process of the King penguin is worthy of medieval royal courts. Over a prolonged period of time, sometimes up to two years, penguins will practice the art of courtship, which involves the wooing of a female with a number of ritualized displays. Here, a female keeps her suitors at bay before closely inspecting her chosen male.

◀◀ **MAGELLANIC PENGUIN BEHAVIOUR**
Magellanic penguins are unusual in that they do not have
a traditional colony but are found in widespread areas
of burrows. The burrows are actively defended from
neighbours and would-be intruders. The ownership of a
burrow is advertised far and wide by the bird's distinctive
call, which gives it its local name of 'Jackass', as it sounds
like a braying donkey.

RE-ESTABLISHING BONDS ▷

Magellanic penguins form very strong bonds with their mates. The bond is re-affirmed every day when returning to the burrow, by touching beaks and bodies as well as mutual grooming.

ROCKHOPPER COURTSHIP ▽

Courtship between Rockhopper penguins is much like that of other penguins, involving specific displays and plenty of calling. Not the most tuneful of calls, the Rockhopper's courtship song is more of a blood-curdling screech. Interestingly, Rockhopper penguins tend to return to their breeding sites year after year and arrive almost precisely to the day. This is unusual given the potential annual changes in weather conditions and food abundance.

A YOUNG KING PENGUIN TRIES TO MUSCLE IN ▲
Often a younger male, or one that has lost its mate, will attempt to interfere with an established breeding pair during their courtship. This can lead to aggressive slapping with the flippers and can escalate to a proper fight – they are even known to draw blood if males are equally matched.

MALE POSTURING ▷
A female King penguin surrounded by suitors. The successful male will be the one who can perform the best ritualized neck-stretching posture over a period of days.

◀ BACHELORS ON THE BEACH
Penguins that are either unable to get a mate or are too immature will sometimes hang out in bachelor groups. Well away from the main breeding colony, they vie with each other and observe intently the tricks of wooing a female.

SYNCHRONICITY ▶
The courtship ritual involves synchronized neck-stretching as well as bowing, trumpeting and finally touching with beaks, necks and feet.

COURTSHIP DISPLAY ▲
Once a potential mate is chosen, or when re-acquainting herself with her former mate, the female King penguin will join the male in an elaborate courtship display.

◄ MATING HABITS

During courtship, the male will position himself over the neck of the female while clacking 'sweet nothings' into her ear with his beak.

▲ KING PENGUIN INTERCOURSE

Eventually, intercourse begins. People often say that you can only tell a female from a male King penguin by the muddy footprints on her back, which is a good indication for the uninitiated.

STRONG PAIR BONDS

King penguins have some of the most intriguing courtship behaviour. The close bonds between breeding pairs allow us to observe moments of real intimacy, exposing their unique characters and endlessly endearing personalities.

◀ SHORT-LIVED MONOGAMY

Female King penguins are ready to mate again just a month after successfully raising a chick. This is much sooner than the male, which can cause some confusion. The pair will be monogamous for the single breeding season but are unlikely to breed together again.

KING PENGUINS MOULTING AFTER BREEDING ▶

After successful chick rearing, or if not breeding, King penguins will moult out their old feathers before returning to the sea to feed. Constant preening ensures that this land-bound process is over as quickly as possible. While moulting, birds will stand together in groups leaving huge piles of feathers behind them.

▼ LESSONS IN LIFE

Despite being reasonably solitary compared to other penguins during the breeding season, Magellanic penguins do congregate to go fishing. Likewise, youngsters are guided into crèches on the beach and are provided with swimming and fishing lessons from more mature individuals.

STRUGGLE
FOR LIFE

The best word to describe the life of penguins in the Southern Hemisphere is 'harsh'.

◀ ROCKHOPPERS DODGE THE CRASHING WAVES

Why the Rockhopper has chosen quite such a difficult place to live and breed is always astonishing. Not only do they raise their offspring on the most precipitous of rock ledges but they climb sheer rock faces in order to reach them. Nature has however, equipped them admirably for this remarkable existence.

A DAREDEVIL LANDING ▶

To cap it all Rockhoppers will often shun the nice soft landing of a sandy beach, preferring instead the terrifying whirlpool of thunderous waves to arrive back on land.

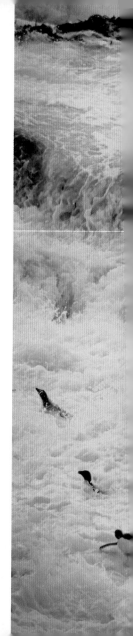

A DANGEROUS GAME ▶

This dramatic image clearly demonstrates the enormity of the task
for the diminutive Rockhopper penguin in going out to sea every
day to feed.

▼ ROCKHOPPERS BRAVING THE WAVES

To watch these creatures being buffeted around in the violent surf, only to
be thrown onto the rocks, leaves you with your heart in your mouth. How
they then manage to gather themselves up and climb, apparently unhurt,
back to their colonies high above is astounding.

◀ ROCKHOPPERS TRY TO AVOID BECOMING LUNCH
Even once back on dry land, the path back to the colony is not without its hazards. Hurriedly zig-zagging their way in tight groups past Fur seals, these Rockhoppers could easily encounter the wrath of the sleepy seals.

A PATH BESET WITH PERILS ▶
When landing on beaches with large numbers of Fur seals in residence, finding a good route back to the colony is quite a challenge for the Rockhoppers.

◀ **INCLEMENT WEATHER**
The ever-present winds and sandstorms can also make the journey to and from the sea difficult for penguins. Leaning into the wind these Gentoos struggle back to the colony, getting thoroughly filthy in the process. Note the outstretched flippers used for balance in the strong winds.

Survival in Antarctica is difficult for all creatures and this image shows the
stark reality of the cycle of life. The Striated Caracara is a rare bird of prey
and an opportunity for a meal is never squandered.

The Leopard seal is one of the most ferocious predators of the Antarctic ice floes. With its reptilian-looking head and a fearsome set of teeth and jaws, a penguin would be a small snack to this extraordinary mammal. About the same size as an inflatable boat, the Leopard seal will actively hunt young and inexperienced penguins around the coastline.

A SKUA SURVEYS THE COLONY ▶

Penguin chicks are also vulnerable to the ever-present Skua. An aggressive but beautiful bird, it is a specialist at stealing penguin eggs from inattentive parents, clearing up carcasses and taking exposed chicks. They will often be found lurking on the peripheries of colonies, scouting the area on the look out for a potential meal.

128

BEACHLIFE

All over the world, life's a beach when it comes to penguins. Even the mighty Emperor penguins are tied to the coastal fringes of the Antarctic continent, all be it some way from the open sea. The beach is the transition point between the land and the sea, the two realms in which penguins live out their complex and ultimately fascinating lives.

GENTOOS ARRIVE ON THE BEACH
Watching the surf for penguins is a time-consuming business. We waited for several hours to see the first of these Gentoos emerge as specks upon the golden sands of this particular beach.

AVOIDING DANGER

Surfing is more fun with your friends, as these Gentoos show. Exploding onto the sand ensures that the penguins get as far up the beach as possible and away from the dangers of the waves and the predators that lurk beneath them, such as seals and sealions. To human eyes, however, it seems that they are also really enjoying themselves.

◀ A GENTOO MIS-TIMES HIS LANDING
Just to prove that it doesn't always go to plan.
This individual spectacularly 'wipes out' on the
beach – a rather undignified landing on this occasion.

SURFERS WITH MORE STYLE ▶
Landing can be done with somewhat more grace and
elegance, as these Gentoos demonstrate – riding the waves
with such skill as to take any spectator's breath away.

With peaks of activity at dawn and dusk, penguins can be found coming and going to and from the sea throughout daylight hours.

▼ **A SNOOZE IN THE SAND**
During the frenetic breeding season penguins are constantly on the go. With long periods of egg incubation and then raising their chicks, it can be an exhausting business.
Sleep is in scarce abundance and so a chance to nap on the beach and do a little sunbathing is rarely passed up.

▲ **A LONE GENTOO PENGUIN STARES OUT TO SEA**
In the chaos of reaching home and timing your arrival on the beach, penguins sometimes appear to lose their friends in the mêlée. Towards dusk, individual penguins can occasionally be seen standing staring out to sea. The reason for this behaviour is unclear but from a human perspective it looks very much as if the penguin is waiting in hope of the late arrival of one of his friends, but perhaps on this occasion Antarctica has claimed another victim.

◀ ESCAPING THE WAVES

During the breeding seasons penguins stay close to their colony sites, but in winter they may drift, along with their food resources, for several hundred miles in and around sub-Antarctic waters and the continental shelf.

GENTOO PENGUINS GATHER ON THE BEACH ▶

Although they do not make their colonies on the beach, Gentoo penguins, from our observations, do spend considerable amounts of time there – recovering and sunbathing on their return from fishing trips. Perhaps they are just delaying getting back to the hustle and bustle of the colony.

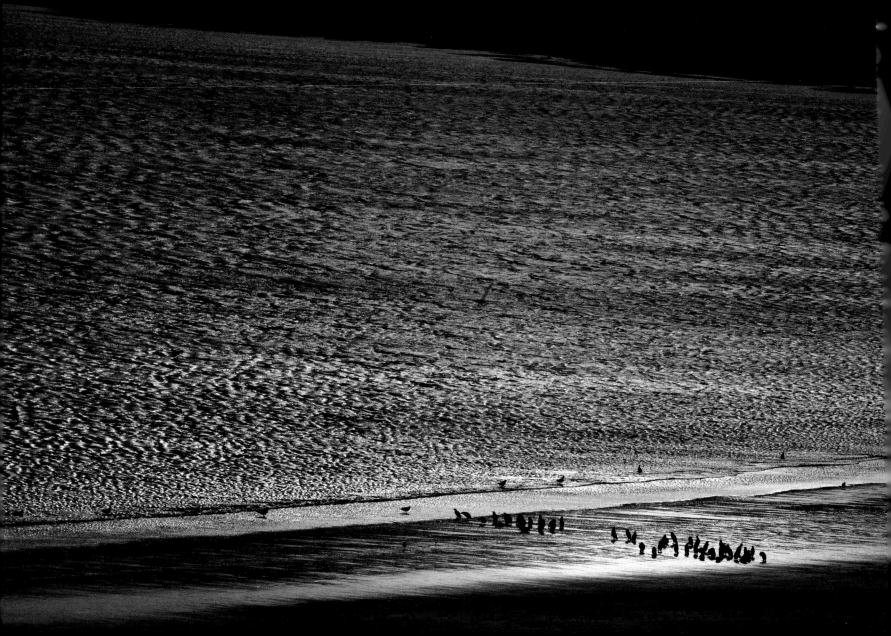

◄ THE ENORMITY OF THE OCEAN

This image really puts penguins into perspective with their environment. They are tiny birds that have adapted to the conditions of Antarctica by learning to exploit the food-rich waters. Their adaptation to underwater flight as opposed to airborne flight has seen them trade lightness for a fatter physique to keep them warm in this freezing environment.

◄ BLUBBER BENEFITS

The blubber, which acts both as a buoyancy aid and insulation for the penguin, has, in the past, made them vulnerable to exploitation by man. They were hunted for their oil alongside whales in sub-Antarctic waters – an industry which has, thankfully, long gone.

KING PENGUINS GO DOWN TO THE ▶ SEA FOR A BATH

Winds are a constant feature of the Antarctic climate. These King penguins are off for a quick bath to rid their feathers of sticky grains of sand whipped up on the beach.

A GENTOO COMES CLOSER ▼

Despite their sporadic persecution by man in the past, penguins have curious personalities and cannot help but to come and take a closer look, especially if you are a photographer with an interesting-looking tripod, camera and lens that you can see yourself in.

◄ **PENGUINS JUST WANT TO HAVE FUN**
Before surfing, penguins will ride up and down within the wave, peering out to see if the coast is clear before ganging up with friends and making a jet-propelled dash for the surf, exploding from the sea and landing on the beach.

REPEAT PERFORMANCE ▶
If the beach is safe, and as far as we can see for no other reason than for practise or fun, they will go back out into the surf and do it all again, and again, with spectacular results.

148

PENGUINS ENJOYING THE BEACH
Penguins seem to enjoy hanging around on the beach – morning, noon and night.

◄ A BRAVE KING PENGUIN TESTS THE WATERS

We spent a wonderful few weeks camping out under the stars on the beaches with these King penguins. We soon found that although tolerant they still looked at us with complete disgust unless we approached on our hands and knees.

◄ THE EARLY BIRD CATCHES THE FISH

Putting his toe in the water, this King penguin is the first to take the plunge this morning, but the others will soon follow.

AN ALTERNATIVE FORM OF FLIGHT
They say that penguins are flightless but one look at them in the water and you can see that they do fly – just not through the air. There are no other birds that can match the prowess of a penguin in swimming and surfing.

THE ENDURING APPEAL OF PENGUINS

Penguins are fun. That, in our experience, is the
only way to describe them. With highly individual
personalities and unique characters they are
awe-inspiring birds that hold a unique place in
the natural world. Their lives are peppered with as
many twists, turns and potential catastrophes as
any one of the human polar explorers of this frozen
continent, and yet to their credit they continue to
enthral us all – especially those of us who have had
the pleasure of their company in the wild.

ANDY ON PENGUINS

My first experience of penguins was one of love at first sight. I sat on a beach, being battered by the incessantly biting wind, as wave after wave of Gentoo penguins surfed onto the beach in front of me. They didn't just swim, they surfed. I smiled constantly, and have smiled ever since when working with them, which is not something that can always be said in the stressful and competitive world of wildlife photography.

It was Christmas Day as I sat alongside a colony of breeding King penguins, just about to call it quits for the day when a kerfuffle broke out as two juveniles burst forth from the crowd. Looking ludicrous in their half-chick/half-adult plumage they came flapping straight towards me. Squeaking all the time they circled me, flippers flapping furiously as if they were trying to take off; I fell about laughing and was crying so much that I couldn't take any shots. That is the power of penguins.

When I am working with penguins I feel really at one with nature, and watching their daily struggle for survival in one of the harshest environments on earth makes me realize how powerless they are to control their own destiny. It is not the penguins that are destroying their environment, it's us. Global climate change is here to stay and we should each do all that we can to reduce its effects globally to ensure that penguins are here for generations to come. Penguins are depending on us – let's not let them down.

For signed books, prints and a lively blog visit the website – www.andyrouse.co.uk

TRACEY ON PENGUINS

Penguins are such enchanting birds and so familiar to us in the western world, even though they herald from some of the most southerly points on the globe. For those of us in the UK they will forever be linked to a favourite chocolate biscuit or with childhood visits to the zoo.

Penguins are not misrepresented by their comical caricatures – they are hilariously funny creatures to watch, probably because of their upright stance and similarity to the way we sometimes behave. I love them.

It is hard to say which species of penguin is my favourite, as I have yet to fulfil my ambition of meeting them all. One of my most memorable experiences has to be when I was sitting on the edge of a Black-browed Albatross colony on the Falkland Islands. I had what can only be described as a 'stinking' cold and at the same time was fighting an attack of vertigo on the clifftop. While peering through the viewfinder I saw something move out of the corner of my eye and turned to see that a gang of Rockhopper penguins had sidled up alongside me, viewing me quizzically. The first in the marching line stopped abruptly as the others absent-mindedly ploughed into the back of him. Indignantly picking themselves up and brushing themselves down, they couldn't resist a closer look, edging nearer to peck at my boot and nip at my sleeve – suddenly I felt a whole lot better.

ACKNOWLEDGMENTS

Ian & Marion Moncrieff, Captain Nick Lambert RN, the crew of HMS *Endurance*, Connie Stevens, Tony & Kim Chater, Susan & David Pole Evans, Rod & Phyll Tuckwood, Rob and all at Sealion Island, Lynn McGonigal, David & Annie Woods, Mark Carwardine, Neil Baber at David & Charles, Andrew Jackson and all at ACTPIX.

All the images in this book were taken with either the Canon EOS 1Ds MK2 or the EOS 1D MK2 and a variety of lenses from 17mm to 500mm. Paramo directional clothing kept us warm while Jobo GigaVu downloaders kept our images safe and sound. Images were processed using Adobe software and no manipulation was undertaken with the exception of minor adjustments to exposure, contrast and saturation.

REFERENCES

McGonigal, D & Woodworth, L (2001), *Antarctica – The complete story*, The Five Mile Press, ISBN: 1-8650-3541-6